TOURISM:

THE BEAUTY OF AFRICA

THE BEST PLACES TO SPEND QUALITY TIME IN AFRICA

BY

ADAM FREEMAN

TABLE OF CONTENTS

INTRODUCTION

Africa is the world's second-biggest and second-most crowded landmass, after Asia in both cases. At around 30.3 million km² including adjoining islands, it covers 6% of Earth's complete surface region and 20% of its territory. With 1.3 billion individuals starting around 2018, it represents around 17% of the world's populace.

Africa has been one of my favorite continents for my travels. I remember some time ago, my friends and I were boasting about Africa and some of the things that struck my heart were the "wide life and beaches". Africa is known as a tourist destination due to its beautiful wildlife, beaches, and culture.

Another thing was that, among other continents in the world, Africa is blessed with so many natural resources, weather, and other things as well.

Without thinking twice about your choice of visitation in Africa, I am glad to unpack different countries I have been to and have experienced. Don't stop reading; there are many things you can learn even if you don't want to visit; you can help others who do. Remember that *knowledge is power.*

By Adam Freeman

Chapter 1

BEST PLACES TO VISIT IN AFRICA

Africa may not necessarily register on the normal explorer's radar, but the people who visit get the opportunity to encounter the ideal mix of antiquated and current, wild and metropolitan, and East and West. To assist you with beginning and arranging your adventure,I've positioned the ideal getaway destinations in Africa in terms of openness, reasonableness, and the range of activities and well-qualified feelings.

Africa is home to dozens, make that hundreds, of public parks, game stores, and other safari attractions. Every single one of them brings something to the table, whether it be a cast of magnetic huge vertebrates overwhelmed by the Big Five, the chance to follow gorillas or chimpanzees, or more inconspicuous joys like searching for uncommon cases or bright butterflies.

Be that as it may, for first-time guests pondering precisely where to go, the features below stand apart as maybe the ten most ideal getaway destinations in Africa.

1. TANZANIA

It is an East African country with a diverse range of natural life.It is well known for its incredible parks like the Serengeti and Ngorongoro Caverns, all popular for safari. Tanzania is home to the Big 5 and numerous other wild creatures.

The absolute best attractions in Tanzania incorporate the extraordinary wildebeest relocation, Ngorongoro pit, Mt. Kilimanjaro, and Zanzibar. The nation has a long shoreline offering incredible sea shores. It is additionally near the equator, giving it a great climate all year.

In Zanzibar, just off the coast, is a fascinating archipelago with flawless sea shores and warm seas. This fabulous area is one of the top vacationer locations in Africa in light of the fact that, for some purposes, it is the ideal spot for the ideal, loosening up ocean side occasion.

With an energetic history tracing all the way back to the seventeenth century, the objective has a supernatural mix of Arabic, Middle Eastern, Moorish, and Indian societies and styles, making it exceptional like no other spot in Africa.

Most vacationers head to Tanzania to go on safari, and you'd be delinquent in the event that you didn't save time to see the country's different fortunes. Notwithstanding its creature-filled fields, Tanzania flaunts extraordinary natural wonders, including red-toned Lake Natron, Ngorongoro Conservation Area's sweeping pit and Mount Kilimanjaro—the tallest mountain in Africa (and the biggest unsupported mountain on Earth). For a definitive adrenaline rush, book a get-over journey up the mainland's most popular mountain through a nearby visitor administrator.

Serengeti National Park (Tanzania)

The Serengeti is Tanzania's longest-running and largest public park.It is engraved as a UNESCO World Heritage Site to a great extent by virtue of facilitating the world's most tremendous yearly natural life movement, containing up to 2,000,000 wildebeest, as well as a huge number of zebra. The extensive fields have Africa's biggest lion population, assessed at 3,000 people. It is likely the most solid spot in East Africa for cheetahs, while panthers are routinely seen in the focal Seronera Valley. Other normal natural life incorporates elephants, bison, giraffe, spotted hyena, bat-eared fox, and a wide assortment of gazelles.

In **Zanzibar**, just off the coast, is an extraordinary archipelago with perfect seashores and warm seas. This incredible area is one of the top traveler attractions in

Africa because, for some purposes, it is the ideal spot for the ideal, unwinding ocean side occasion.With a lively history tracing all the way back to the seventeenth century, the city has an enchanted mix of Arabic, Middle Eastern, Moorish, and Indian societies and styles, making it remarkable like no other spot in Africa.

When to visit ?

There's no terrible time. From June to October, offers incredible general natural life viewing as well as a valuable opportunity to see the wildebeest migration.The wildebeest calve from late January to February. Many recurrent guests favor April and May, when the field is at its greenest, rack rates drop, and vacationer volumes are at their most minimal.

Where to stay?

There are many midrange to upmarket cabins and risen camps in the Serengeti, as well as a few camping areas.

My group and I lived it up there. The views and treatment were actually extremely fascinating. It is a superb place to visit. The best chance to visit is around June to October.

2. MADAGASCAR

For get-aways, Madagascar is one more country in Africa appropriate for voyagers searching for harmony, wonderful sea shores, and extraordinary nature. It is encircled by the Indian Ocean and has incredible inns and resorts of top-notch level. The nation has a long shoreline with baobab trees, clean sea shores, and marine life. Madagascar is likewise home to a few public parks, giving one a combination of beachfront life and untamed life experience.

Longing for a tropical escape spent relaxing on ideal islands, traveling across verdant rainforests, climbing around stunning stone developments and spotting remarkable untamed life? Then, at that point, put your focus on Madagascar. Situated in the Indian Ocean, around 743 miles east of Mozambique, this African paradise is the fourth biggest island on the planet. Roughly 19,000 sorts of plants can be tracked down in the country's 47 public stops and saves, but its exceptional creatures are the primary draw for nature darlings. The world's 100 or more lemur species call this island country home, as do in excess of 340 sorts of chameleons and different birds.

However, you'll probably invest some energy in crowded regions like Antananarivo (the nation's capital) and Nosy Be (a little island off the central area's northwest coast). Madagascar is loaded up with districts ready for investigation. Explorers can make a beeline for a swim around Nosy Sakatia or swim at The Three Bays, and photography fans can snap stunning photos of the sun rising or setting over Morondava's Avenue of the Baobabs. In the meantime, approach the climbing trails at Anja Community Reserve, in addition to Tsingy de Bemaraha Strict Nature Reserve's transcending limestone zeniths, which are great for climbing. On the off chance that you'd prefer to have a more quintessential Malagasy excursion, travel deep into public parks like Isalo and Mantadia to watch lemurs, boa constrictors, and seriously wait in the trees.

3. SEYCHELLES

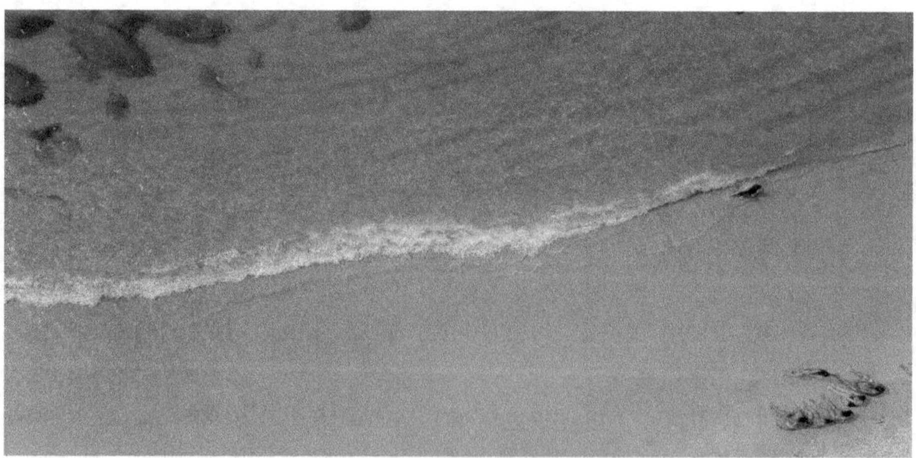

Seychelles is the littlest country in Africa and is made of 115 islands. The nation is 1,500kms from central area Africa. It is a country with extraordinary uninhabited normal locales. It is a lovely country with immense rich rainforests, mountains, valleys, coral reefs, rives, and marine life.

With the country's 115 islands, there is such a huge amount for a traveler to appreciate. It offers spotless, delightful, and disconnected sea shores that sightseers can appreciate during an excursion. Exercises might incorporate swimming, scuba plunging, riding into the mountains, and boat trips.

Whenever troubles arise, the extreme get moving — and most of us summon our ideal departure, longing for a distant island with swarm free sands, radiant blue waters and a peaceful air. However, when you're prepared to transform that fantasy into a reality, put your focus on Seychelles, a group of 115 islands peppering the Indian Ocean off the eastern bank of Africa. You might have gotten a quick look at the landscape here previously: The apparently unending white sea shores, monster rocks and influencing palms are the stuff of postcards, TV plugs and work area foundations. And keeping in mind that you're relaxing along these well known coastlines, almost certainly, the main other living things you'll experience will be the islands' bright birds and humongous turtles.

The Seychelles islands are frequently alluded to in two separate gatherings. Most voyagers limit their investigation to the 43 Inner Islands, putting together themselves with respect to one of the gathering's three principal isles. Mahé is the biggest, home to the Seychellois capital, Victoria, as well as the popular Anse Intendance ocean side. Praslin, the second biggest of the essential islands, likewise flaunts a few acclaimed coastlines, also Vallée de Mai. And afterward there's La Digue, a calm island where bikes rule and the sands of Anse Source d'Argent ocean side stay untainted. Contract a personal ship farther to the ocean and you'll probably find one of the 72 Outer Islands, low-lying, sandy cays controlled by untamed life. It doesn't get more remote than that.

4. Cape Town, South Africa

To the extent that the best vacation spots in Africa goes to Cape Town as a city and its encompassing region is a lot of the simplest and most open method for experiencing Africa all in all.

Cape Town is one of the top traveler objections on the planet, a beautiful blend of individuals, societies, custom, history, nature, and food, it maybe the most ideal way to characterize the Mother City.Here a traveler can investigate top vacation spots in Cape Town South Africa, everything from Robben Island to the notable Table Mountain National Park, Cape Point, Cape Winelands, and Camps Bay, experiencing new mountain air and sea breezes throughout the entire year. Assuming that you make the right move at the right time, you could possibly go to one of the most amazing live events in South Africa. Best time to visit is from November to January. Secret Seasons (best opportunity to be a nearby) are October and late February to March.

Lively, in vogue, shocking, friendly… If Cape Town was an individual, it would be that Hollywood celebrity we as a whole subtly envy. The Mother City is not normal for some other objective in Africa: Separated from the remainder of the mainland by a ring of mountains, Cape Town remains as a sparkling, city compared with one of the world's most stunning regular scenes. However, great looks aren't the main thing Cape Town has making it work. You'll experience passionate feelings for this city's khaki-hued sea shores, moving grape plantations, sizzling food, flourishing nightlife, and, obviously, the breathtaking Table Mountain. It might have taken a worldwide soccer competition to grab the world's eye, yet since Cape Town took the worldwide stage, no measure of humming vuvuzelas can overwhelm its heavenliness. Cape Town is by a long shot the most cosmopolitan city in South Africa, as it has a mixed bag of societies that adds to the city's varied music, food, and celebration scenes. Yet, to more readily value Cape Town as it is currently, it's essential to comprehend what the city has encountered. Many years of racial and financial mistreatment conjured by politically-sanctioned racial segregation has left a rotting wound. Albeit numerous vacationers just experience Cape Town's dazzling sea shores and energetic cafe scene, the people who visit Nelson Mandela's prison cell on Robben Island or scrutinize the displays in The District Six Museum will see that there's a serious suggestion to this generally lively city.

5. Maasai Mara National Reserve, Kenya

At the point when individuals consider Africa, they consider wild creatures and safaris. The Massai Mara

National Reserve in Kenya is one of the best 10 vacation spots in Africa, and each traveler has a decisively unique encounter when they visit.

The Massai Mara is one of the main 10 vacation spots in Africa, to consider well as experience the large 5 but since of the wildebeest movement. Going on through the Maasai Mara National Reserve will lead you to the Serengeti National Park and Game Reserves in Tanzania. There are numerous expert voyages through this noteworthy nature hold and with an assortment of game survey encounters from ordinary overland vehicles to hot air balloons.Essentially the Kenyan partner to the Serengeti, the more modest Masai Mara is similarly remunerating with regards to game review. Enormous felines are the star inhabitants. Prides of up to 20 lions hoard the spotlight, however it is likewise a generally excellent spot to see cheetah and panther, alongside elephant, bison, giraffe and - with a smidgen more karma - dark rhino. The Masai Mara makes its mark over late July to early October, when a huge number of wildebeest show up from the Serengeti to cross the Mara River, the most tremendous piece of the yearly movement.

Amboseli National Park (Kenya)

When individuals consider Africa, they consider wild creatures and safaris. The Massai Mara National Reserve in Kenya is one of the best 10 vacation spots in Africa, and each traveler has a decidedly unique encounter when they visit.

The Massai Mara is one of the top ten vacation spots in Africa to consider if you want to see the Big 5 but because of the wildebeest migration.Going on through the Maasai Mara National Reserve will lead you to the Serengeti National Park and Game Reserves in Tanzania.

There are numerous expert voyages through this noteworthy natural area and with an assortment of game survey encounters, from ordinary overland vehicles to hot air balloons. Essentially the Kenyan partner to the Serengeti, the more modest Masai Mara is similarly remunerating with regards to game viewing. Enormous felines are the star inhabitants. Prides of up to 20 lions hoard the spotlight, but it is likewise a generally excellent spot to see cheetah and panther, alongside elephant, bison, giraffe, and-with a smidgen more karma-dark rhino. The Masai Mara makes its mark from late July to early October, when a huge number of wildebeest show up from the Serengeti to cross the Mara River, the most tremendous piece of the yearly movement.

Amboseli National Park (Kenya)

The world's tallest unattached mountain and the heftiest, earthly well-evolved creature are the critical attractions of Amboseli National Park. It is from here that one acquires the most motivating perspective on snow-covered Kilimanjaro as it overshadows the creature-rich fields of East Africa. Amboseli has the world's longest-running elephant study, laid out in 1975, and it is one of the most mind-blowing spots to visit in Africa to see communication between elephants, which are curiously very much acclimated and stunningly tusked here. It is likewise an extraordinary birding objective because of its blend of occasional swamps and semi-dry acacia savannah.

The best chance to visit is during the virus season from July to October, when the game review is great consistently. Be there between late August and early October to be sensibly sure of getting the wildebeest movement. Some other time is best in the event that low vacationer volume means a lot to you.

Where to stay?

Many midrange to upmarket cabins and rose camps are spread in and around the Masai Mara. A few campgrounds can be found within its boundaries; they are reasonable and agreeable.

6. VICTORIA'S FALL

Outdoorsy sorts head out all over to appreciate this amazing UNESCO World Heritage Site. Riding the boundary between Zambia and Zimbabwe, Victoria Falls is generally two times as profound and wide as Niagara Falls, making it one of the world's greatest cascades. To see this normal marvel at its heyday, plan a visit in April, when the district's stormy season has finished up. Well known vantage points incorporate the Knife-Edge Bridge, Livingstone Island, and Devil's Pool. At the point when you're despising the view from a higher place, go whitewater boating in the Zambezi River to respect the tumbles from an alternate point.

The falls in Zimbabwe and Zambia are something everybody has found out about, and for the majority, what African dreams are loaded up with. Victoria Falls is a mutually owned vacation spot that can be seen and explored from either Zambia or Zimbabwe.

A great 108 meter high fountain of water, frequently called "The Cloud that Thunders", isn't only one of the top vacation destinations in Africa but the world. Victoria Falls is a hypnotic and remarkable top ten vacation spots in Africa that is on many people's bucket lists.The Zambian side of the falls has higher tourist traffic, and it's in a city called Livingstone, Zambia. Thus, in the event that you would prefer a more loosened up experience, visiting the Victoria Falls on the Zimbabwe side will be a superior fit.

The Victoria Falls town is effectively walkable, so vacationers can stroll between the shops, cabins and workmanship markets at their souls' substance.

The town is essentially built for travelers and has the look and feel of an amusement park. Victoria Falls town likewise has the different necessities any city would have-general stores, bistros, amazing cafés. Concerning convenience, the Victoria Falls Hotel is within strolling distance, and other incredible spots to remain are effortlessly reached by transport or cabs.

As you pass through from Victoria Falls Airport or Hwange Street, you'll get a brief look at the spray from Victoria Falls on your right side. The splash, from a good way, seems as though a fog is framing a fleecy looking cloud. It's no big surprise that Victoria Falls means "the smoke that roars" in the Tongan language. As you continue towards the town, you'll be welcomed by monkeys from the roadside, and in the event that you're fortunate, maybe they'll be invited by an elephant. Since the untamed life is permitted to meander openly around Victoria Falls Town, most creatures regularly avoid regions with heavy traffic and are not perilous whenever let be.

7. CAIRO, EGYPT

The desert heat, the uproarious roads, and the sheer size of Cairo will leave even the most versatile explorer with a serious case of culture shock. The steady siege of roadside vendors, the inevitable fragrance of animals, and the apparently tumultuous lifestyle will wiggle the faculties. Yet, show restraint. Make time to unwind over a cup of tea, wander the ancient roads, and watch the sun set over the mighty Nile River.It won't take long for the city's fortunes to reveal themselves.

Most guests rush to Egypt's cash-flow to investigate the marvels of the old world, following the strides of the pharaohs. In any case, there are different sides to Cairo; the city's occupants embrace their set of experiences and cheer for their advancement. The antiquated pyramids of Giza, Dahshur, and Saqqara battle with the popular bars of the Zamalek and Heliopolis neighborhoods for the spotlight. Sounding taxis strive for space with whinnying jackasses on the thin roads. What's more, the customary Islamic call to petition, relaxing music, and tumultuous chitchat can be heard all the while. The best way to get a genuine feeling of Cairo is to mix the old with the new.

Giza Necropolis, Egypt

Many individuals don't consider Egypt to be in Africa. In the Giza Necropolis, you will get to see the Great Pyramid of Giza, the Pyramid of Menkaure, and the Pyramid of Khafre.

Giza Necropolis, Egypt:

The Giza Necropolis must be something on many travelers' lists of must-dos. The old Egyptian human advancements are resurrected along the Nile through pyramids and burial places. Not the Africa that most people think of, but certainly a part of Africa that everyone should visit. The best times to visit are from October to April, when temperatures are cooler.

8. THE KALAHARI DESERT IN AFRICA

From the primary hints of human existence by the Khoisan nation to an unparalleled safari experience, Kalahari gives an outline of Southern Africa basically.

The desert is considered the best spot in Africa to see cheetahs in nature. The Kalahari's completely open scenes permit you to effectively see the cheetah, dark maned lion, panther, and jeopardized African wild canine in real life.

A large portion of Southern Africa is hidden by vast deserts, but none of them is as active as the Kalahari, which covers 360,000 square miles.In spite of possessing tremendous regions in Botswana, portions of Namibia, and Northern South Africa, the Kalahari is difficult to squeeze into a solitary profile.

Every country has its own environment and soil, so Kalahari has a variety of veneers for every path.It was not only home to the most unusual wild life in Africa, but it was also a watcher of movements and settlements dating back millennia.

Map of the Kalahari Desert

You can perceive how huge the Kalahari Desert is from the guide as it rules most of the Southern African nations on the west coast of the mainland.

It rides the Tropic of Capricorn, and it is transcendently hot and humid at a height of around 1000 m above ocean level.

A guide to the Kalahari Desert

Interesting Kalahari Desert Facts

Here are a few fun facts about the Kalahari Desert:

Considering how everyone calls it a desert, you may be stunned to learn that Kalahari is certainly not a genuine desert. This is related to the yearly precipitation of 5–10 inches, which is excessively high for the normal dry season in Africa.

The word Kalahari comes from the Tswana word Kgala, meaning "incredible thirst." This is in light of the fact that the Kalahari sand totally assimilates the water and leaves nothing on a superficial level.

Kgalagadi Transfrontier Park in the southern Kalahari is Africa's most memorable peace park, one of numerous that expect to rise above man-made boundaries and save untamed life.

The earliest occupants were the Khoisan nation, who lived as tracker-finders. Upon Bantu's relocation, their country was involved with ranches worked by Bantu individuals. This made it challenging for them to support their ways of life, which many of them had proactively absorbed. With the arrival of European pioneers, new disputes arose.Today, there are still countless San individuals in the Kalahari locale. In any case, the San public are engaging against the Botswana government, who are attempting to move them to different regions of the country.

Kgalagadi Transfrontier Park.

Kgalagadi is described by dark red sand ridges and camelthorn trees inside a huge semi-dry sandy landscape of 3.6 million hectares. Kgalagadi is unique in Southern Africa.

The recreation area possesses regions in Botswana, Namibia, and South Africa, so you can in fact enter each of the three nations in a single visit. The feature is the beautiful game drive through the parched landscape with a grand game review, including Black-Mane Lion, cheetah, panther, Hyena, and an inconceivable number of impalas.

Begin saving your thoughts

The sand hills are sufficiently high as all encompassing post places, so you can do a great deal of invigorating hunter watching.

Focal Kalahari Game Reserve

Focal Kalahari contains the biggest game hold in Botswana and the second biggest by and large with 52000 km square kilometers. You could find the limitlessness a piece overpowering; fortunately, the directed safari visits know where to take you with pinpoint exactness.

Every one of the wild creatures you can imagine are found meandering openly, including dark maned lions, wild canines, cheetahs, panthers, jackals, bat-eared foxes, African wild felines, zebra, giraffes, and great many birds and bugs.

The untamed life is grouped in the northern finish of the recreation area inside Deception Valley, so the drives will probably take you there.

Still not persuaded about the uniqueness of this public park? Maybe social trips into the existence of nearby San occupants will adjust your perspective. The fabulous grandkids of the primary Kalahari Bushmen actually live here in their crude ways and rehearsing their practices.

You could not just observe their day to day routines at any point yet in addition see antiquated rock workmanship to widen your insight about them.

Makgadikgadi Pans

A salt skillet is an immense level region covered with salt and minerals, framing through fast vanishing of water pools in deserts.

Kalahari is a one of a kind objective with wonderful topographical circumstances and a fast dissipation rate. In this way, finding the biggest salt skillet of Africa, Makgadikgadi Pan, in the Kalahari wouldn't surprise.

It was beforehand the Makgadikgadi Lake with a size bigger than whole Switzerland. Stone devices extricated during the unearthings in Makgadikgadi demonstrated the presence of ancient man nearby.

Today, it is home to invigorating natural life of wildebeest, zebra, and hunters like lion, cheetah, and Hyena. You can experience the bunches of creatures coming to hydrate from puddles or join memorable paths directed by relatives of agrarian Bushmen.

Augrabies Falls National Park

The word Augrabies in Khoisan signifies "clearly thunder," which is generally exact for a huge sheet of water tumbling from 60 meters.

The falls situated in a serene corner of the Northern Cape offers every one of the treats concealed in the region. Different post focuses to see the cascade can be combined with hot air expanding, wine sampling, and watersports in the Orange River.

Best Kalahari Desert Accommodations

The following is a rundown of convenience choices giving an agreeable stay and simple admittance to the critical exercises through coordinated visits.

The northern piece of Kalahari has surface water, consequently more bountiful in untamed life. It's feasible to find a lot of the three African huge felines (lion, panther, and cheetah) in one spot.

The southern part contains more dry adjusted species like springbok, gemsbok, wildebeest, kudu, duiker, Hyena, and meerkat.

The birdlife is bountiful in ostriches, Kori bustard, hawks, goshawks, kestrels, and secretary birds. Reptiles are generally found all through, including the harmful Cape cobras, puff adders and reptiles.

The vegetation is very different, contingent upon the environment. The southern locale is incredibly dry, and it contains bushes and hedges impervious to dry season. It seems to be a desert because of the wealth of Hoodia cactus. Eatable plants and vegetables that require a modest quantity of water can be developed here, like cucumber and melon.

The focal Kalahari gets more downpour and suits the development of a bigger number of trees, particularly Acacia species, camelthorn, blackthorn, shepherd's tree, and silver bunch leaf.

9. Etosha National Park (Namibia)

Namibia's lead save, Etosha is overwhelmed by the huge, saline and regularly dry prospect it is named. The container is lined by a progression of enduring waterholes - some floodlit around evening time - that draw in huge crowds of gazelle, giraffe and other slow eaters during the dry season. It is additionally one of the more dependable parks in Africa for dark rhino, which happen here close by lion, panther and elephant however not bison. Etosha is curiously very much equipped towards self-drive safaris.Otherworldly scenes anticipate in postcard-commendable Namibia. In this southern African nation, you'll find the shockingly gorgeous Namib (the world's most seasoned desert), in addition to public parks lodging various fascinating creatures (like zebras and springbok) and sea shores ignoring wreck filled waters. At the point when you're not investigating the striking red ridges of Sossusvlei or the dead camel thistle tree-filled Deadvlei - the two of which can be found in the Namib - search for rhinos in Etosha National Park and partake in a rough terrain visit through the Skeleton Coast. Likewise save time to encounter the European style of Namibia's previous pilgrim towns, like Lüderitz and Swakopmund.

At the point when you can visit Etosha: Game review is great all through the dry time of April to October, and tops over July to September.

Where you can remain: notwithstanding the reasonable government-run rest camps sited inside the recreation area, a few additional selective camps and hotels stand right external it.

10. MOROCCO

I accept that supported tips and counsel will assist anyone with first stumbling to Morocco run as flawlessly as could really be expected - while partaking in its best sights.

Morocco is a magnificent touristic nation and one of the most well known traveler objections out there. It is a cordial vacationer nation and one that makes certain to intrigue each voyager. It has dazzling mountains, delightful shorelines, old urban communities, extraordinary culture, and the immense sand ridges of the Sahara Desert.Let's talk about the absolute most famous things to see and do in Morocco as well as a things to keep an eye out for and decorum.

Fez Or Fes

Fez is one of the biggest urban communities in Morroco and one of the country's primary traveler objections. Fez is an exceptionally extraordinary city for a scope of verifiable and engineering reasons and has been named the "Famous hub of the West" and the "Athens of Africa." Fez is an UNESCO World Heritage-recorded site and a flat out must-see on any excursion to Morocco. One of the fundamental attractions of Fez is the Medina Of Fez.

Marrakech

Marrakech (or Marrakesh) is southward and inland in Morocco. It is the doorway to the Sahara. Here you will feel like you are in a customary and a desert garden desert city. Marrakech is very much set up for the travel industry and its desert and Mediterranean engineering is a wonder to view. The business sectors, food, and markets here are outstanding.

One thing to remember. In Morocco, to snap a photo of somebody's shop or execution, it's supposed to tip or possibly purchase something.

Tangier

Tangier is the scaffold among Spain and Morocco, you can undoubtedly take ships this way and that from here. Tangier has an exceptionally gorgeous old city worked around the old strongholds. Here you can see probably awesome of Morrocan design and culture. Tangier is a waterfront city and from the sea shores, you can look across the mouth of the Mediterranean to Spain and Gibraltar around 15 miles away.

For a roadtrip, visit the Caves Of Hercules only 9 miles out of Tangier. These noteworthy precipice side caverns manage the cost of an incredible perspective on the mouth of the Mediterranean.

Casablanca

Casablanca is popular for the old-fashioned 1942 film of a similar name. This is a delightful city and certainly worth a visit. As well as having a lovely old downtown area, Casablanca is something of the New York of Morrocco and is the main monetary and useful city. Casablanca likewise has the most active air terminal in the country. It is surely worth going through a little while in this memorable city.

Rabat

Rabat is the capital city and is somewhat less touristy than different urban communities. However, it is certainly worth a visit. Here you can see the customary business sectors and the old waterfront palace. It merits going through a day in the capital, Rabat.

Something significant you should be cautious about is that;While Morocco is a protected nation, be careful about cellphone burglary. Be cautious about utilizing your cell phone in the city and assuming you do, attempt to utilize it away from the road and in your grasp inverse the road. It is entirely expected for motorbikes to descend the road and grab your telephone out of your hand.

The choice is yours to make, but make it fast so you can enjoy any of the above best destinations.

Chapter 2

Brief History About Tourism In Africa

During my years of research, I discovered some histories behind tourism; which I would love to share with you. My colleagues and I had a wonderful experience trying to figure out some of these materials in other to help travelers understand why tourism is an important aspect of the human life. It is a source of happiness and helps to build confidence, meet new people, learn new things and culture. I never wanted to do this, until my wife talked me out of it, and now am having the best experience in the world. Tourism is another dimension where an individual has the opportunity to explore the nations across the world, it's not something one would love to miss, and if you are missing this please pause a bit and have a rethink about tourism. So, now let's dive into some of the brief histories about tourism in Africa. There's no place like Africa in the world for wildlife,wild terrains and rich customs that persevere. Plan to fall head over heels. I've had the option to investigate new nations all through the African landmass — from the deserts of Morocco to the pyramids of Egypt, from the Giraffe Manor in Kenya to Victoria Falls in Zimbabwe also,

Zambia, and particularly the bramble of South Africa. There's an experience sitting tight for you on the mainland of Africa!

Tourism is a significant financial area for some nations in Africa. There are numerous nations that benefit vigorously from tourism like Uganda, Algeria, Egypt, South Africa, Kenya, Morocco, Tunisia, Ghana and Tanzania.The touristic identity of Africa lies in the wide assortment of focal points, variety and large numbers of scenes as well as the rich social legacy.

The mainland of Africa can be partitioned into three gatherings comparative with tourism:

- those nations with a created tourism centers;
- those with a creating tourism centers;

- those that might want to foster tourism centers.

Nations like Morocco, Egypt, South Africa and Tunisia have an effective tourism. Nations like Kenya, Zimbabwe, Eswatini and Mauritius can be considered as nations that have consistent and steady pay from tourism. Nations like Algeria and Burundi are nations that have practically no monetary advantage from tourism however might want to see it grow.

The effective nations in tourism are flourishing because of various elements. Nations like Morocco and Tunisia benefit from their lovely sea shores and their general closeness to Europe. Tourism in Egypt depends on the rich history of Ancient Egypt, pyramids, relics and stunning Red sea shores. South Africa and Kenya benefit from wild safari campaigns, drawing in sightseers to see the natural life of Africa. Its a whole lot of fun I must say, this is not what you should ever miss out.

When did the tourism in Africa begin?

The tourism started during the 1800s, while Europeans making what was known as the "fabulous visit" of Europe started stretching out their movements to incorporate more extraordinary objections. MOROCCO, ALGERIA, SOUTH AFRICA, and particularly EGYPT and the NILE RIVER valley pulled in numerous European guests.

Africa has been one of the world's quickest developing the travel industry districts, growing a little base of just 14.7 million guests in 1990, to 26 million worldwide travelers in 2000 and 56 million in 2014.International vacationer appearances in Africa are assessed to have expanded by 2% in 2014. In outright terms, they locally invited a sum of 56 million worldwide tourists. Africa's 2% ascent anyway addresses an unmistakable log jam on tourism interest following quite a while of strong growth. International the tourism receipts (+3%) expanded by US $1 billion to arrive at US $36 billion. They locally kept 5% offer in overall appearances and a 3% share in the travel industry receipts.In North Africa (+1%), worldwide vacationer appearances in driving objective Morocco became by an unobtrusive 2%, following areas of strength for an in the earlier year, while appearances in Tunisia diminished by 3%.Sub-Saharan Africa became by an expected 3% in 2014, in light of accessible information. Arrivals to the sub district's biggest objective South Africa (+0%) were level in 2014. Worth focusing on among different objections for which information is accounted for are Côte d'Ivoire (+24%), Madagascar (+13%), Mauritius (+5%), Zimbabwe (+3%) and the Seychelles (+1%).While numerous nations in Africa profited from solid monetary development in their tourism area, the landmass' portion of overall tourism receipts is generally unobtrusive.

Tourism makes occupations and invigorates SME (Small

also, Medium Sized Enterprise) development. In 2014 it addressed 9% of world GDP - immediate, roundabout and actuated influence.

Tourism is one of the quickest developing areas of the world economy. Worldwide Tourism has shown practically continuous development since the 1950s and has nearly multiplied over the past decade.Tourism shows specific commitment for creating nations. Tourism is filling quicker on the planet's arising and creating districts than in the remainder of the world. Tourism speeds up change, it is a guide for favorable to business arrangements and changes that can help SME advancement and animate unfamiliar venture.

Chapter 3

IMPORTANCE OF TOURISM IN AFRICA

Tourism offers numerous chances to put resources into Africa's rich nearby networks, produce financial movement, and set up business opportunities for ladies and youngsters. By 2030, customer spending on neighborliness and entertainment in Africa is projected to reach about $261.77 billion. The significance of tourism to work in Africa is developing. While the area accounted for only 11,600 positions in the district in 2000, this number increased to 20,500 in 2014 (8.1% of all employment in the district).Between

Between 2008 and 2011, the quantity of positions diminished; since then, at that point, it has been expanding consistently. As per the World Travel and Tourism Council (WTTC), touristic commitment to work is supposed to develop to 26,000 in 2015. With respect to tourist direct commitment to business, the advancement has been comparable, and from 2000 to 2014, the area acquired very nearly 3,500 new positions straightforwardly connected with tourism.

Tourism offers numerous chances to put resources into Africa's rich nearby networks, produce financial movement, and set up business opportunities for ladies and youngsters. By 2030, purchasers' spending on neighborliness and entertainment in Africa is projected to reach about $261.77 billion.

It has prompted the advancement of the workmanship and specialty industries in light of the fact that privately made things like drums, crates, and mats are offered to unfamiliar guests (visitors).

It assists in enhancing the economy, consequently lessening reliance on horticulture and guaranteeing a consistent capital stream.

It assists with effectively utilizing inactive land, consequently diminishing asset wastage. For example, *Kidepo Valley public park.*

It has set out to open doors for individuals in Africa, prompting further developed ways of life, for example, game officers, local escorts, travel planners, e.t.c.

It has worked with the improvement of frameworks like streets, which help in the development of labor and products in East Africa.

The public authorities procure income through tax assessments from individuals who work in the travel industry, which is utilized in the improvement of streets.

Tourism is an imperceptible commodity which procures the public authority unfamiliar with trade utilized for the advancement of foundations, for example, streets.

Tourism prompts the advancement of global connections, which helps in advancing world harmony and laying out world solidarity.

Tourism assists in preserving the climate and safeguarding normal magnificence, which is significant for the present and people in the future.

Chapter 4

WHY SHOULD I COME TO AFRICA?

Typically, the main justification for travelers' visits to Africa is to set out on a natural life safari or climb Kilimanjaro. While Africa absolutely has the most productive untamed life, seeing open doors and one of the seven culminations, there are some more "other" motivations to head out to Africa.

The African mainland abounds with special scenes, antiquated history, geological marvels and dynamic undertakings for sure.Look at different motivations to visit Africa that will take this unbelievable mainland leap toward the main spot on your experience list.

1. Tropical sea shores that rival a portion of the world's ideal.

Africa positively has a ton of seashores, making it difficult to pick something truly mind-blowing. Nonetheless, a top pick would be the shores of the sea on the little island of Zanzibar, simply off the shoreline of the Tanzanian capital of Dar es Salaam.This little island flaunts clear sky blue waters, white coral sand and a lot of plunging and swimming opportunities, making it the ideal spot to loosen up after a safari or journey up Africa's most elevated peaks, Mount Kilimanjaro and Mount Kenya.

2. Lively urban areas

Africa is a blend of old and cosmopolitan urban communities.

Investigate Morocco's Marrakesh, a thickly pressed, middle-age city that traces all the way back to the Berber domain. The labyrinth of back streets and flourishing business sectors inspires pictures of Disney's Aladdin, and you'll be frustrated, shaking the picture of an enchanted rug from your psyche as you peruse many unpredictably hand-woven floor coverings from the diverse souks.Conversely, South Africa's Cape Town is a cutting-edge cosmopolitan city that flaunts a fabulous shoreline and a rich social legacy and history. The city is undeniably beautiful, both for its setting against one of nature's new seven wonders, Table Mountain, and for its rehabilitation of modern locales, Dutch, Malay, and British-influenced engineering, and notable structures.

3. Topographical marvels

Visit the world's most noteworthy sand dunes in the Namib desert; witness the world's biggest and most impressive cascade, Victoria Falls, in Zambia and Zimbabwe; and investigate the rich water universe of the Okavango Delta in Botswana.

Find Ngorongoro Crater, a UNESCO World Heritage Site of the world's biggest whole, un-overflowed volcanic caldera, or even visit Fish River Canyon, the second biggest stream ravine on the planet (after the Grand Canyon).

With a great assortment of untamed life, culture, and experience, the African mainland will offer genuinely extraordinary encounters.

4. Setting up camp, glamping, and in the middle between.

Setting up camp in Africa is an empowering experience; it offers a close association with the land, nature, and untamed life (we're talking birds and scarabs-not bison and lions). All in all, what better way to have a really vivid method for encountering Africa?

The best thing about setting up camp in Africa is that there are many grades of setting up camp, so it's not all hedge tents and basic necessities—although there is that as well! Whether you're enthusiastic about setting up a shelter to encounter the outside direct, need that tad of extravagance, similar to shrubbery showers joined to your campground and completely overhauled setting up camp, or very good quality setting up camp in rich vault tents with full sheet material and an ensuite, Africa offers everything.

5. Make a beeline for the waters for an alternate safari experience.

However, not generally connected with the nation's dry scene, there are energizing water-based exercises, including investigating the untamed life-rich Okavango Delta by mokoro, and kayaking down the Manambolo River in Madagascar, overflowing with endemic birds. Enter the dynamite and little-visited Manambolo Gorge through a limestone level. It's an incredible option in contrast to the typical game drive safari experience.

In the event that your inward water-kid requires an excursion with water exercises, Africa has all you want and the sky is the limit from there.

6. It's overflowing brimming with BIG things.

As the second greatest landmass on the planet, Africa is jam-loaded with a portion of the world's greatest things:

• The biggest desert on the planet, the Sahara Desert (investigate it on our Morocco agendas).

• The longest stream on the planet, the Nile River, runs for 6,853km (4,258mi).

• The world's greatest inland delta, Okavango Delta (see it on our Botswana schedules).

• Most noteworthy unsupported mountain on the planet (and one of the Seven Summits), Mount Kilimanjaro (ascend it on our Kilimanjaro journey).

• The world's most seasoned desert - the Namib desert in Namibia (see it on our Namibia undertakings).

• The world's biggest natural life movement on Earth happens in The Serengeti in Tanzania, with more than 750,000 zebra walking in front of 1.2 million wildebeest as they cross this special scene (experience it on our Serengeti Explorer).

• It's the home of the biggest residing land creature, the African elephant, which can gauge as much as seven tons.

• You'll likewise find four of the five quickest land creatures here - the cheetah (70 mph), wildebeest, lion, and Thomson's gazelle (around 50 mph).

• It has the world's most broad open air craftsmanship exhibitions with more stone workmanship destinations than some other landmass. Huge sums have been found in the Sahara Desert, Namibia, Zimbabwe, Kalahari and Botswana. Be that as it may, many stay unseen since they are arranged in distant region of the desert or are seldom visited by people. The most established realized craftsmanship viewed has been assessed as between 27,000 - 40,000 years of age, offering an understanding into the old individuals' convictions, lifestyle and stories.

7. More than 3000 interesting clans and societies

Africa is home to more than 3000 clans, each with unimaginably varied dialects, societies, and customs.

Some of the clans are notable: the Zulu, which likewise is Africa's biggest ethnic gathering of 11 million individuals; the Masai, who have well-established customs and culture and are known for carrying on with an itinerant way of life and crowd-steering professionally; and the San and Batswana individuals of the Eastern Kalahari, with a social legacy that is more than 20,000 years old.

While thousands more exist, each has similarly interesting networks and customs that spellbind the advanced world.

individuals, the [illegible], who have well-established customs and culture, and are known for carrying on with a [illegible] way of life and [illegible] professionally, and the Samburu [illegible] of the Eastern [illegible]

[illegible]

Chapter 5

POSSIBLE DANGERS TO AVOID

While remaining protected in Africa is generally a question of sound judgment, there are a few locales or nations that are really hazardous for tourists. In the event that you're currently arranging an outing to Africa and aren't certain about the security of your picked objective, it's really smart to check the movement alerts given by the U.S. Division of State.

What Are the Travel Warnings?

Travel admonitions or warnings are given by public authorities trying to admonish U.S. residents about the risks of going to a particular region or country. They depend on master assessments of the country's ongoing political and social circumstances. Frequently, travel alerts are given as a reaction to prompt emergencies, for example, nationwide conflict, fear-mongering assaults, or political overthrows. They can also be given in response to rising social distress or rising crime rates, and they can occasionally reflect health concerns (for example, the West Africa Ebola epidemic of 2014).

As of now, tourism warnings are positioned at a size of 1 to 4. Level 1 is "practice ordinary precautionary measures," which basically means that there are no extraordinary security worries as of now. Level 2 is "practice expanded alert", and that truly means that there is some gambling in specific regions, but you ought to in any case have the option to travel securely for however long you're mindful of the gambling and act in like manner. Level 3 is "reevaluate travel", and that implies that everything except fundamental travel isn't suggested. Level 4 is "don't travel," and that implies that what is happening is excessively perilous for vacationers.

For more information about the conditions that move individual travel admonitions, consider checking the warnings given by different legislatures, including Canada, Australia, and the United Kingdom.

Current US Travel Advisories for African Countries

Below, we have given an outline of the tourism warnings for all African nations with a Level 2 position or higher.

Please note that movement alerts change everything all the time, and keeping in mind that this article is refreshed routinely, checking the U.S. is ideal. Visit the Division of State site straightforwardly prior to booking your outing.

Algeria

Because of psychological oppression, a level 2 tourism warning has been issued.Psychological oppressor assaults can occur unexpectedly and are seen as more logical in rural areas.The admonition especially cautions against movement to rustic regions inside 50 kilometers of the Tunisian boundary, or inside 250 kilometers of the lines with Libya, Niger, Mali, and Mauritania. Overland travel in the Sahara Desert is additionally not recommended.

Burkina Faso

Tourism warning level 3 issued due to wrongdoing, hijacking, and illegal intimidation.Rough wrongdoing is far-reaching, especially in metropolitan regions, and frequently targets far-flung nationals. Psychological oppressor assaults have occurred and could happen again out of the blue. The warning raises the country's ranking to Level 4 for a few areas, including Arrondissement 11 in Ouagadougou and 11 districts in the Sahel, Cascades, and Boucle du Mouhoun regions.

Burundi

A level 3 tourism warning was issued due to wrongdoing and political savagery.Savage wrongdoings, including projectile assaults, are normal. Irregular viciousness happens because of increasing political pressure, while police and military designated spots can confine opportunities for development. Specifically, cross-line assaults by equipped gatherings from the DRC are normal in the territories of Cibitoke and Bubanza.

Cameroon

Because of wrongdoing, a level 2 tourism warning has been issued.Rough wrongdoing is an issue all over Cameroon, albeit a few regions are more terrible than others. In particular, the public authorities exhort against all movement toward the North, Far North, Northwest, and Southwest areas as well as portions of the East and Adamawa locales. In a portion of these areas, the opportunity for psychological warfare and equipped struggle is likewise elevated.

African Republic in Focus

A level 4 tourism warning has been issued due to wrongdoing, widespread distress, and abduction.Outfitted burglaries, kills, and exasperated attacks are normal, while furnished bunches control enormous regions of the nation and frequently target regular people for kidnappings and killings. Unexpected terminations of air and land borders in the event of common turmoil imply that vacationers are probably going to be abandoned assuming difficulty emerges.

Chad

Tourism warning level 3 issued due to wrongdoing, illegal intimidation, and minefields.There has been an expansion in detailed vicious violations beginning around 2018, while fear-based oppressor groups move effectively all through the nation and are particularly dynamic in the Lake Chad locale. Lines might close abruptly, leaving travelers abandoned. Minefields exist along the lines of Libya and Sudan.

Côte d'Ivoire

Because of wrongdoing and psychological oppression, a level 2 tourism warning has been issued.Fear mongering assaults might happen out of the blue and are probably going to target vacationer regions, particularly in the northern boundary district. Vicious violations (counting carjackings, home attacks, and furnished burglaries) are normal, while U.S. government authorities are restricted from driving outside significant urban communities into the evening and can hence give restricted help.

Vote-based Republic of the Congo

Because of wrongdoing and general unrest, a level 3 tourism warning has been issued.There is an elevated degree of savage wrongdoing while political shows are unstable and frequently unlawful, an outrageous reaction from policing. The eastern Congo and the three Kasai territories are given a Level 4 position because of their continuous outfitted struggle. North Kivu and Ituri regions are likewise Level 4 because of wrongdoing, Ebola, and kidnappings.

Egypt

Because of psychological warfare, a level 2 tourism warning has been issued.Psychological militant gatherings keep on focusing on tourist areas, government offices, and transportation centers, while common avionics is viewed as in danger. A considerable lot of the country's principal vacationer regions are moderately protected, notwithstanding. In the meantime, travel toward the Western Desert, the Sinai Peninsula (with the exception of Sharm el-Sheik), and the boundary regions isn't suggested.

Eritrea

Level 2 tourism warning issued due to movement restrictions, limited consular assistance, and landmines.Assuming you are captured in Eritrea, almost certainly, admittance to U.S. government office help will be denied by nearby policing. Landmines are a gamble in numerous remote as well as rustic regions of the nation, including (but not restricted to) Nakfa, AdiKeih, and Arezza.

Ethiopia

Level 2 tourism warning issued due to the possibility of common agitation and resulting disturbances.Going to the Somalian boundary region isn't exhorted because of the potential for seizing, psychological warfare, and landmines. Outfitted struggle as well as common agitation are additionally viewed as probable in regions, for example, the East Hararge district of Oromia state, and the borders with Kenya, Sudan, South Sudan, and Eritrea.

Guinea

Because of widespread distress, a level 2 tourism warning has been issued.Political showings happen every now and then and are frequently flighty. Before, some have brought about serious wounds or fatalities, while protestors are probably going to target drivers who endeavor to go through or around combat activity. Sharp criminals might focus on the people who become caught in the clog brought about by shows.

Guinea-Bissau

A level 3 tourism warning has been issued due to wrongdoing and widespread distress.Fierce wrongdoing is an issue all through Guinea-Bissau, particularly at the Bissau air terminal and at Bandim Market, the focal point of the capital. Political agitation and social brokenness have been continuous for a really long time, and struggle between groups can make brutality erupt whenever. There is no U.S. government office in Guinea-Bissau.

Kenya

Tourism warning level 2 issued due to wrongdoing, psychological oppression, and capturing.Savage wrongdoing is an issue all throughout Kenya, and vacationers are cautioned to keep away from the Eastleigh and Kibera areas of Nairobi consistently, and to practice alert while going out into the evening. The Kenya-Somalia line, a few beachfront regions, and portions of Turkana County are positioned at Level 4 because of the risk of psychological oppression.

Libya

Tourism warning level 4 issued due to wrongdoing, psychological warfare, equipped struggle, capturing, and general agitation.The possibilities of becoming involved with vicious radical action are high, while fear-based oppressor groups are probably going to target far-off nationals (and U.S. residents specifically). Common avionics is under attack from fear mongers, and flights throughout Libyan air terminals are consistently cancelled, leaving tourists stranded.

Malawi

Because of widespread agitation, a level 2 tourism warning was issued.Recently, planned political exhibitions have occurred in metropolitan areas across the country.Defacing and plundering frequently go with these fights, and cops have been known to answer with brutal techniques, including the sending of nerve gas.

Mali

Tourism warning level 4 issued due to wrongdoing and psychological warfare.Brutal wrongdoing is normal all throughout the nation, particularly in Bamako and the southern districts of Mali. Barricades and irregular police checks permit degenerate cops to exploit vacationers going on the streets, particularly around evening time. Fear monger assaults keep on focusing on places visited by outsiders.

Mauritania

Tourism warning level 3 issued due to wrongdoing and psychological warfare.Fear-based oppressor assaults might happen suddenly and are probably going to target regions visited by Western vacationers. Savage wrongdoings (counting burglaries, assaults, attacks, and muggings) are normal, while U.S. government authorities should get exceptional consent to go beyond Nouakchott and can thus give restricted help in instances of crisis.

Morocco

Because of psychological warfare, a level 2 tourism warning has been issued.Fear-based oppressor groups keep on arranging assaults in Morocco and may target tourist locations and attractions as well as open vehicle center points. These assaults are eccentric and may happen with next to zero advance notice. Voyagers are encouraged to stay away from shows and groups where possible.

Niger

Tourism warning level 3 issued due to wrongdoing, psychological warfare, and abduction.Brutal wrongdoings are normal, while fear-mongering assaults and kidnappings target unfamiliar and neighborhood government offices and regions visited by travelers. Specifically, keep away from movement to the boundary locales, particularly the Diffa district, the Lake Chad area, and the Malian line, where fanatic gatherings are known to work.

Nigeria

Tourism level 3 warning issued due to wrongdoing, psychological oppression, common agitation, abduction, and robbery.Brutal violations are normal in Nigeria, while psychological oppressor assaults are especially common in the upper east. The provinces of Borno, Yobe, and northern Adamwa are positioned at Level 4 because of the danger of psychological warfare. Robbery is a worry for explorers of the Gulf of Guinea, which ought to be stayed away from.

The Republic of the Congo

Because of wrongdoing and general agitation, a level 2 tourism warning has been issued.Savage wrongdoing is a worry all throughout the Republic of the Congo, while political exhibitions happen habitually and frequently turn brutal. Vacationers are encouraged to reexamine travel toward the southern and western locales of the Pool Region, where continuous military tasks bring about a higher gamble of common distress and outfitted struggle.

Sierra Leone

Because of wrongdoing, a level 2 tourism warning has been issued.Brutal violations, including attacks and theft, are normal, while neighborhood police are seldom ready to actually answer calls. U.S. government workers are restricted from going outside Freetown into the evening, and can hence just provide limited help to any travelers that wind up in a difficult situation.

Somalia

Tourism warning level 4 issued due to wrongdoing, psychological warfare, seizure, and robbery.Fierce wrongdoings are normal all over, with continuous unlawful road obstructions and a high rate of kidnappings and murders. Fear-based oppressor assaults target Western vacationers and are probably going to happen abruptly. Robbery is overflowing in the worldwide waters off the Horn of Africa, particularly close to the Somalian coast.

South Africa

Level 2 tourism warning issued due to wrongdoing, widespread unrest, and a dry spell.Vicious wrongdoings, including armed burglary, assault, and crush and-snatch assaults on vehicles, are normal in South Africa, particularly in the CBDs of significant urban communities into the evening. Political fights happen every now and again and can turn vicious. The Western, Eastern, and Northern Cape regions are encountering a serious dry spell and water limitations might apply.

South Sudan

Tourism warning level 4 issued due to wrongdoing, capture, and furnished struggle.Equipped clash is continuous between different political and ethnic gatherings, while rough wrongdoing is normal. The crime rate in Juba is particularly low, with US government officials typically only permitted to travel in heavily armed vehicles.Limitations on true travel outside Juba imply that vacationers can't depend on help in a crisis.

Sudan

Tourism warning level 3 issued due to wrongdoing, psychological warfare, common agitation, seizure, and equipment clash.Individuals from realized fearmongering groups dwell in Sudan and are probably going to target Westerners. Viciousness is normal along the boundaries with Chad and South Sudan, while furnished resistance groups are dynamic in the Central Darfur, Blue Nile, and South Kordofan states.

Tanzania

Level 2 tourism warning issued due to wrongdoing, psychological oppression, medical issues, and the targeting of LGBTI travelers.Savage wrongdoing is normal in Tanzania and includes rape, hijacking, robbing, and carjacking. Fear mongers keep on arranging assaults on regions visited by Western travelers. In September 2019, informal reports were put forth with respect to the defense of Ebola in Dar es Salaam.

Tunisia

Because of psychological warfare, a level 2 tourism warning has been issued.Certain regions are viewed as more in danger of assault than others. The public authorities exhort against movement to Sidi Bou Zid, the desert south of Remada, the region of the Algerian line and the hilly regions in the northwest (counting Chaambi Mountain National Park). Going inside 30 kilometers of the Libyan line is likewise not suggested.

Uganda

Because of wrongdoing and capture, a level 2 tourism warning has been issued.Although numerous areas of Uganda are viewed as somewhat protected, there is a high frequency of fierce violations (counting outfitted burglaries, home intrusions, and rapes) in the country's bigger urban communities. Travelers are encouraged to take special consideration in Kampala and Entebbe. Neighborhood police miss the mark on assets to answer really in a crisis.

Zimbabwe

Because of wrongdoing and general unrest, a level 2 tourism warning has been issued.Political unsteadiness, monetary difficulty, and the impact of the ongoing dry season have prompted common turmoil, which might manifest itself through fierce exhibits. Brutal wrongdoing is normal and common in regions visited by Western vacationers. Guests are informed not to show apparent signs of abundance.

Countries at Level 1 with High Risk Areas

The accompanying nations have been given a general Level 1 position, yet incorporate regions with a higher degree of risk: Angola, Benin, Gabon, The Gambia,

Ghana, Liberia, Madagascar, Mozambique, Rwanda, Senegal, and Togo.

Despite all the bad things said concerning Africa, it's still the world's best tourist center. It is a place full of adventures, lots of natural resources, and the *beauty of nature.* My candid advice to you reading this book is that you shouldn't allow fear to hold you back from the world's greatest adventures. Africa is called *the "World's Wonder,"* and this is because of the fascinating things about Africa. I want you to take your time and explore the world's hidden truths. Africans are the nicest set of human beings. They can render their best.

Long ago, during my stay in South Africa and Tanzania, my team and I were happily welcomed and well fed with their traditional meal. We all enjoyed it. We had countless hours of assistance from those civilians. Africa is an amazing place to visit.

About The Author

Adam Freeman is a globetrotter. He has travelled to different countries across the world. His love and support for humanity has brought him closer to unveiling the most relevant thing for every individual, and that is tourism. He has left his shoes in countries such as the United States, Canada, Dubai, Botswana, Egypt, and many others. He believes that nature is calling him to come and experience it. He is from Finland and has helped many people achieve their goals; he has three children and a lovely wife. This book is one of his best African experiences, and he has written other books.

www.ingramcontent.com/pod-product-compliance
Lightning Source LLC
LaVergne TN
LVHW050317160826
845677LV00014B/3442

9798845840509